The
Branding
Blueprint

A GUIDE FOR

musicians, entrepreneurs, and small business owners to execute marketing strategies

CORY AUSTIN

The Branding Blueprint

The Power of Digital Branding

Copyright © 2020 by Cory Austin

First Printing 2020

Published by

Imperial Media Design

The Branding Blueprint:

The Power of Digital Branding

If you're not familiar with me, let me fill you in about my background. I'm Cory Austin, and I've also gone by the name Defiance as a music artist. I've been a Music/Digital Media Marketer for over 10 years. What you are reading is my introductory book, *The Branding Blueprint - The Power of Digital Branding.* It's an insightful guide written to help music business professionals, who are new to digital marketing and advance their techniques in the realm of media.

In addition to my marketing background, I also have over a decade of experience in the music industry. I have tapped into my marketing skills and music industry experience to compile a book that will equip you in **implementing a solid and sophisticated marketing plan**. This is labeled a cheat sheet for music business professionals, and these same techniques can apply to any small or medium size business. Through my dynamic understanding, I'll provide the following tools:

- **How to make more money with less effort.**

- **The hidden success secrets of independent business owners.**

- **How to scale your company into profitable creative business.**

- **Top pitfalls that every successful entrepreneur should avoid.**

This book does not go into music law, contracts, types of revenue models, fan fair or anything of that manner. Rather, this is very practical marketing techniques. The contents of this book heavily weigh into email and its correlation with other supportive digital marketing strategies.

My insight comes from my many years of sales and hard-hitting hustle. Having this self-taught discipline also inspired me and gave me the drive to consult large corporations, but more so with small businesses and entrepreneurs I learned the needs of the local companies and how each of them differs from marketing on a large scale. I have contracted my services as director for various large vaping distributors, managing and building international marketing departments.

I have assisted in product development and launches within the cannabis industry. My background includes over 10 years in the consumer electronics industry curating global relationships with brokers in China, Russia, Saudi Arabia, Canada and the U.K. My public relations (PR) background involves celebrity endorsements and marketing strategies in the world of music. During my entrepreneurship in music, I have consulted as a media director for Freeway Rick Ross's Team called "Young Freeway Nation," and all the way to solidifying business advice from P Diddy's Dirty Money Group. I am handing over the information I studied, obtained and applied first-hand.

I don't have all the answers, but through my experience, my goal is for you to leave with more information than you started. I offer approaches that can impact your business and creatively evolve your strategies for the long haul.

An Intro to Email and Digital Marketing

D o you know that over 34 percent of humans throughout the globe use email? That is close to three billion people because of a prediction of over 300 million users every two years. This is to show you the power of the Internet and email. Again, let me shock you! Do you know that 196 billion emails are sent every 24 hours?

The amazing thing is—109 billion of the 196 billion emails sent daily are business associated emails.

Now, imagine all these three billion beautiful users receive a well-crafted email about your organization, every day. Do you think it will impact greatly on your business?

What if a huge chunk of those 109 billion business mails was from your company?

Think about it, there is an untapped energy in electronic mail. It can work wonders for your business.

The truth is, this form of marketing is a tangible and effective way to reach your prospects. If you think I'm bluffing, how many people do you know who don't have online mail? Almost virtually everyone receives some type of message in an inbox. Whether we agree or not, email has now been identified as a necessary tool. The facts speak for themselves.

Email is a unique customized way of reaching your clients or your prospects.

That's why email marketing works so well. You have the chance to personalize your message. Your email can be adjusted to the individual's peculiarities and needs. Three billion users are a whole lot of blessings, don't you think?

If you're still thinking that email marketing is not something for your company, then let me give you a few reasons why it's is a platform you wouldn't want to underestimate:

Marketing has become the key element in being able to push and promote any business and product. You have probably heard the word "marketing" endlessly from various directions in the last several years. This is because it's true, it's a key element. Marketing is like a centipede with many different legs, a catch-all phrase for several different avenues and each effective in its own process. With the growth of social media and content marketing, information sharing has been introduced at an all-time high.

While information thrives in being shared on the digital front, the intimacy between individuals and content producers have dwindled. Even with social media making information readily available.

The learning curve has been lowered with such little emphasis placed around true valuable information. There is a void and disconnect, and people are missing the direct communication of personal interaction. Marketers are still using traditional media forms to reach their audience online with and without social media. This allows high value information to be produced and distributed, without conflicting against modern competing content. We will be covering one of the most effective means of digital communication outside of social media, which is email.

Email is a word that many feel has almost become antiquated, but it's not. Tens of thousands of people daily are still using email to share, educate and grow their business across vast networks. Email marketing allows you to build long-lasting solid relationships, while supporting value behind the content that you choose to promote. Only using email to promote is good but is not enough on its own. I want to discuss how to create full-fledged marketing campaigns through email distribution and automated systems.

Emailing can be a single one-off function or a systematic campaign that integrates with several moving parts. Email marketing in itself has several layers to peel back. I find it important that we study more than one perspective of email marketing in order to grow our fan bases. If you're a musician or a music business professional, you'll want a large amount of value placed on loyalty.

Email is right for you if you're thinking about connecting with individuals on a personal level. Social media has been great in many aspects but also has its limitations. When you think of connecting with people, social media has done this in an open forum. Allowing content to be shared and broadcasted over large arenas to engage audiences in a very broad manner. Social media will allow you to circulate just enough number of words for the infinite number of the ideal sets of persons. This proves to be very effective, but in a day and age where social media is the medium for most marketing, email still holds a relevance in space.

Emails afford readers the mindset of ownership, given that they can afford to read your message and not delete it by dropping it in a trash icon right away.

The right copy written information can be psychologically genius—amazingly, with this sense of ownership, they are more likely to read your message as soon as they see it. Email marketing gives you an insight into customer's behavior and comprehension of the type of content they would likely respond to. This is definitely more effective than the traditional method of marketing. The email list has proven time and again to be the advertisement winning card of an ideal business. Reason being is that you're provided with a set base of contacts, which you can continually sell your services or products to in repetition. Of course, given that you have valued content that meets the needs of people in your list.

Email is only a click away, taking only a split second to deliver, whether the receiver is down the street or other side of the globe. As a result, you are able to observe the status of your ads in less time than the traditional marketing methods. As a result, the repeated flow of information makes room for increased productivity amongst the staff in an organization. In addition, it also makes room for rapid improvements and adaptability when emergencies arise.

Email messages will always remain in the recipient's mailbox, except when they deliberately delete it. But not all hope is lost. You'll have the opportunity to send additional emails, giving you a second chance to change the recipient's mind and win them over. Why not get the most out of your website? This is indeed the blazing trail.

The entire point of your email marketing is to promote your business and encourage prospects to see the power of your website. As mentioned, social media has done this in an open forum and allows content to be shared and transmitted to large-scale platforms with an intent to engage audiences. Social media will allow you to spread word to people with a shotgun effect, allowing your message to spread and gain traction from others when done correctly. This proves to be very effective, but in a day and age when social media is the medium for most marketing campaigns, email provides a better, articulated targeting approach.

With email, readers gain a sense of ownership of the content: they can read, delete or save the content. Once they see it, it gives a sense of exclusivity, like receiving a text message. Businesses still pay hundreds of thousands in examining data of opened and click through rates with emails. Email marketing provides information about customer's behaviors and what they are interested in seeing. An email list is a goldmine for any business because you have a list of contacts you can repeatedly sell to, as long as your content is relevant.

What are you currently doing to entice your prospects? If you're a musician, how are you engaging with your fans? Giving value is the flavor of any real campaign. Creating information that is both compelling and draws people in. You have complete control over the curation of content within an email campaign.

You don't have to worry about who the social media platform chooses for content visibility. With social media, algorithms can detect the likes, shares and comments rate within a specific time period. These algorithms decide the level of engagement and visibility that your post will receive.

When you're running an email campaign, the post and social behavior is null and void. Your message completely depends on the terms and conditions of your ISP for not delivering spam and if the recipient of the email finds it compelling enough to open. We will go into the content of the email later.

When you first jump into your email marketing efforts, the first people to pop into your head is contacting friends and family. You want to let people know so they can help your engagement ranking. Usually with engagement of any business and product, from my personal experience, family and friends aren't the best to start with. Family and friends often expect discounts or have preconceived notions about you already, so your expectations may differ from what you expect until you start crossing major milestones.

This doesn't mean you shouldn't share and allow them to know about content you'll be developing. However, your expectation of them supporting the entirety of your business should be eliminated. You'll find that much of your support comes from people who you don't know and people you meet who have no idea about you. This is good because you won't be judged by your faults or your shortcomings, and you can just work off your skill.

You want to engage with new people who don't know you. This is a perfect way for you to create the image you want and the persona that people can remember.

It isn't important what people have known of you because these are not the people who support you. The purpose of dealing with people you don't know is to always have new prospects to engage with, like new fans. The goal is to drive interest from each person to engage in an interactive way.

The Relationship of Social Media

W hy social media? In what way does social media and emails come together? In every way! This is the source you'll capture your emails from. Companies use forms on their social media pages to capture emails. Having content that gives people reason and compels them to want more is what generates email addresses. A musician who has an album they're releasing wants immediate sales, and they want hard work to "pay off." Well to who? Who will you sell your music to? Will you post it on social media and expect everyone to immediately click download or purchase?

It doesn't work that way. Why? One, the oversaturation of information and content creates an information overload. Someone is selling something every time you go online. No one wants to be sold anything, especially if they're not familiar with it. Two, the purpose of capturing email addresses is to bring people into your world—a world you share together that creates a relationship. An artist can't sell an album without an audience or a fan base since it takes time to build a group of people who are interested in what you're selling. But that time can be minimized when it's done correctly.

People on social media platforms are looking for relevant information, which pertains to them. They look for three distinct types of content: education, interactivity or entertainment. That's it. They want these forms of reliable content in order to share and engage frequently. You must build a source of relevant information online for people to want to engage. This is the key. The "Me" Model, won't work. (Unless you are a huge established brand.) The "Me" model is any time when you develop content that's all about your product, and it's off putting. Because all you're thinking about is what you can earn. That is a very failing model. Once again, no one wants to be sold— they want to be social. Right now, when society is experiencing a tumultuous time, it's challenging to persuade people to part with their money online, but once they do, they will continually buy. Why won't they buy from you? Because they don't know you, don't know anything about you, and haven't heard anything proven about what you sell. You haven't given any value or credibility to your work.

You need to create content that is not a part of the "Me" Model. Start developing content that is relevant and engaging for others. Therefore, it's important to know the interest of the demographic you want to target. What do they like? Where are they located?

People do not go to social media to purchase, they are looking for the exact opposite, such as free information, free entertainment, and even free products. Also to socialize and not be removed from doing so.

Useful content is a dime a dozen and great content for free is a flying unicorn. This is what the world wants. How does all this fit into your model? First, know if you have relevant content to fit the audience you are pursuing. You are more prone to have someone click, like, share and comment on something that they can relate to rather than a product you're hoping someone will purchase.

How does free help you? Well, this is the beginning. You have to get the first transaction. The first transaction may not be monetary. It may be the exchange of communication or the exchange of contact information. You give great content for the exchange of contact, which is known as a conversion.

Think of an email address like a phone number in the digital realm. People protect and guard their email to ensure privacy for a reason. An email is personal, and it can be checked from your mobile phone and in private. It can be used for business or personal—it's yours. Content seekers do not like to openly give their email especially on social media sites. Developing content that gives someone a snippet of valuable information with links to click is part of your secret sauce. This is the formula for driving traffic and collecting data.

Using content to develop a following is secured with a strong call to action. You need to have congruence within each piece of content. The content must be useful in some way that is relevant to each engager's interest. This will mean at times creating content that is separate from your products but may hold relevance within your industry. There are thousands of pieces of content on the internet relevant to almost any industry that you can think of. If you do not understand content is king, you will be building an already failed empire. The idea is to create yourself as a cornerstone of information that will propel people to seek more. Soon you will see that your social media followers will begin to grow, and you should have collected the email for most of those followers in some way. Because the next level of transactions will begin after you have moved off the social media platform and into email engagement. You want to get to know this prospect better, and you want them to get to know you better. Dig in and offer more to get more. Your more enticing information will take place within the next stage you exchange.

Chapter 1

Start Digital Branding

Emails are a wonderful way to engage and build relationships with clients, customers or fans. You can email all the information you want, but it helps to break down people into a specific list to receive specific types of emails. Several types of emails are used when delivering content to an audience and speaking to people in diverse ways. Some are very broad while others may be niche. The main ones we'll cover are as follows:

- Newsletters

- Announcements

- Email Blasts

- PR Campaigns

Let's first talk about lists. Once you bring any emails into your database, the first thing you want to do is place them under a list. Lists can determine how you categorize your email prospects based on interests. You can make lists based on their attributes, but interests would be the best place to start. The reason for this is because you can continue to send content to recipients congruent with what they were interested in to begin with. This match in content would be on social media or whatever source you collected them from.

Newsletters, which are a mixture of content consolidated into a single message, are the most common tools and resources that most companies will send subscribers via email. You can receive every news update, entertainment piece, and event listings based on your preferences. It's broad content sent out regarding many different topics. Newsletters can be fun and keep people engaged, and it can also include product sales or services. There isn't any rule to the correct type of newsletter or the content you can put in it. It's your newsletter, so use your discretion. I would recommend this for an audience who has a strong interest with your content or brand. You will want to keep your subscribers' interest with the right content.

Where your meat and potatoes can come into play is with announcements. Announcements are overlooked because they aren't utilized correctly. They are the specific spotlight on one targeted item or newsworthy information within your business. This can be a service or product. This is great because you can build focus and value around one core item. That item will be what gets people's attention. Usually when a single item is highlighted as a sellable product, then you''' want a sales page either built into the email or a clickable link to take the recipient to the sales page. The idea is to build enough value surrounding this product that it justifies the price it's selling for. Announcements could be as small as "website maintenance" or as large as "50% off everything." Once again, it's completely up to you. What you'll need to know is how much power you have in these announcements. You can create a powerful sales tool for any of your products. When it comes to building value, (I know I have said that often) I'll get into it a little later in this book.

Email blasts are a great way to share releases. Instead of targeting a specific list, you can do a full audience release of content. Many times, these are great for musicians. These releases can be content associated with your company but not directly related. If you are a record label or a distributor, you may want to send out an email blast for an album launch or release party. You also may want to announce music projects that you will be working on. Always have your call to action, but be aware that the driving force behind an email blast isn't always sales as much as it is attention. You are making people aware of something. Email blasts can become very lucrative, and after you have built your email list to a certain point, you can also charge other creators to release their content. This service is referred to as selling a drop list. Content being put out to an engaging audience becomes extremely valuable to the right company. People create businesses out of providing this service alone.

Dealing with PR Campaigns can be tricky but beneficial if done right. Any email announcement should just be in support of your PR that you have running. If you want to give your audience exclusivity and transparency, then you can allow them to get a leak of your story or newsworthy content right before you send it off to the media. This way they feel that you recognize their value (and exclusivity goes a long way). When people discover information about a company or brand that they follow from an unrelated news source, it puts them in shock. The stunned feeling is similar to if you've worked at an investment bank and you had a friend who heard on the news that the bank you worked for was going under but you didn't know yet. How would you feel about the company?

So, when you welcome your fans in, make sure they are within a level of your internal family. Now you can create levels to your content in which your diehard fans know exclusive information only given to a selected group and not available to everyone else. This is how you build deep levels of trust and buyer commitment. PR is also a great way to get feedback, which people can give you useful information to apply to your business. On the flip side, be ready for any criticism too. Like I said, PR can be tricky.

Chapter 2

KPI's and Result Tracking

Remember how I was talking about separating and organizing your lists? Well this is a handy process because when you market content, you want to make sure it's what people want. When you stop sending valuable information to your recipients or subscribers, then they will start identifying your emails as spam, causing your open rates to decrease and the possibility of them deleting your messages or unsubscribing from the list. You don't want any of these to happen, but the common outcome of most emails sent will be bounced, deleted or unsubscribed from. That's just the nature of the business; your purpose is to minimize that.

After every campaign, you'll want to check the following: your open rate, click-through rate, how many bounced, and how many went through. A whole slew of ratios. This is going to tell you how engaged your audience is with your content. Do they love it? Is it unrelated? Are the emails they're receiving high-quality? You'll also be able to know how people are accessing your emails, such as by mobile phone, desktop, or tablet. These are important metrics because it describes what devices give you the strongest engagement from your audience. You will want to optimize future content toward the devices giving you the strongest activity. This comes into measuring your KPI's (Key Point Indicators). You'll also want to measure your success based on conversions, and if you see substantial amounts of discrepancies and numbers inconsistent with your goals, then you'll know a variable needs to be adjusted.

Nothing ever rolls out right the first time—it's an experiment. You will want to consistently look at the tracking of each one of your email campaigns and see what works best as far as content. How is it useful for the audience? Having key points become quotas that allow you to know when you have met goals, which will allow you to scale upward or cut back some of your efforts if your goals can't be achieved. Your goals should be reasonable and tracked by conversions, revenue or activity that are attainable and realistic. You should look at the history of progression to forecast what you may want to aim toward.

A process that works well for marketers is A/B testing, which is also known as split testing and refers to two variants: A and B. This is where you send the same content to the same listing with small variations to the subject line or the content. You can determine the style that your audience wants by how engaged they are or from how many may choose to unsubscribe. Don't let unsubscriptions discourage you. It's a process in which people choose to unsubscribe for many different reasons. The good thing is that you can continue to get more. The pond of new contacts isn't going dry any time soon. Split testing will let you know what works for you as a brand. It also lets you know where your dialogue can be stronger. For example, if you owned a sneaker shop and wanted to promote a pair of Nikes that retail $150, then you can split test campaigns into two: one half of your email list receives a promotion for $60 off and another group receives a 40% discount. Both have bold lettering and the only difference is a nuance in the sale promotion. Yet they both come out to the same price. When you go look at the tracking results for your email campaigns, you will see which one is the winner.

Another cordial thing about being an adamant tracker with emails is that you can look at how many click-throughs have occurred. This is going to tell you the amount of link clicks that you received from content in the email. If you have links to anything within the email that directs people to websites, products, content or blog information, then your analytics will reveal all this.

Having your click-throughs will let you know how important people find your content with links and if it's a product you can determine some of your sales based on these links. It's very difficult to run email campaigns with no tracking analytics. It's a blinding experience, like throwing darts in the dark. The less you measure your target, the greater chance you have of missing your bullseye.

Chapter 3

Temperature of Your Prospects

Every successful person in sales has to be able to measure their customers through a buyer's timeline. Knowing exactly what triggers that person to buy at what specific point. Since products vary between industries, so does the fluctuation of when someone chooses to purchase. If you can understand when someone is on the buying path, you won half the battle. Is it an instantaneous sale like an album or a long-term sale like a home? This process is where you want to gauge what your prospect needs when making a buying decision.

The way I want to discuss entering a buyer's timeline is first understanding the temperature of your traffic. When reaching new fans or prospects, there are three distinct temperatures that you will walk a prospect through.

- Cold

- Warm

- Hot

Gauging the temperature of your prospects allows you to know two things, which are when products should be pitched and a person's immediate needs. Everyone that you haven't spoken to or done business with are basically cold traffic. They may be in your industry, but they are cold if they have never heard of you. If people don't know you exist, then no rapport exists. Generally, this makes everyone on social media cold traffic. When it comes to cold traffic, you will want to offer different content than you would for your warm or hot traffic. So, this squanders the idea of selling immediately when you jump on social media. Take the time of getting to know your audience. Who is out there? Who is engaging with you? Who are the people you are extending your reach to?

Cold traffic is like going to the club to pick someone up but not offering a drink or good conversation. The approach entails you know how to flirt with your audience and pique their interest. Take the time to familiarize them with your way of handing out useful information that pertains to your industry. You can use URL tracking services like bitly.com to create links to maximize information. When you share content that will move people from social media, use a bitly.com link to shorten your posts, which can track how many people are clicking on your link and where they are coming from. Cold traffic isn't about trying to close the deal. If you're in a bar, you can't expect to immediately take someone home before getting them interested (depending who you are). You want to get to know them, build chemistry through dialogue and exchange contact information. This is the same method that you'd want to do for cold traffic. Immediately trying to sell is going to be a burn since you'll want to pique their interest first. Cold traffic is going to react better to free content. You build value in information that you give that is relevant to the people in need of it. Free content that's educational, entertaining or engaging. Become relevant to your industry by being a source for people, and in turn, a source for traffic. There is nothing wrong with sharing your product, but it needs to have value mixed onto your timeline as well. Therefore, cold traffic is referred to as the "Activation" stage. This is the time you're activating new clients. Similar to your mobile phone company, you get started when you are activated as a user, and now you have been welcomed into the network. Can you hear me now?

Warm traffic is what most businesses like. Something finally happens when people are paying attention. What did you do differently? Well, you are giving people content they like so they interact in a way you like. It works out. Warm traffic is people that have said, "Okay, I'm interested, and I'm activated. What more can you offer?" This is the "Acquisition" stage. What happens with warm traffic? These are the guys who have now joined your network. They are in your email list, and they want to hear about all the wonderful things you have to offer. With the acquisition stage, you are now actually taking notice to where real conversions are taking place to drive in email traffic. Pay attention to where you are spending most of your effort. When you start seeing email conversions, you'll want to know where you are receiving the largest results. How can your efforts be maximized to grow greater results? Because the warm traffic still isn't about the sale as much as it's about collecting the data.

During this time, you still have new fresh eyeballs on your content, but they haven't purchased anything. However, warm traffic has gotten you one step closer to a paying transaction. In the activation stage, you wanted to lure people in with free content. With warm traffic, you may want to attract potential buyers with low-ticket items, which are tied up in bundles and packages. Selling bundles that offer value for a very rational dollar amount will be your target selling point for warm traffic. Newsletters and announcement emails will work great with getting warm traffic attention. They are looking for great products and interested in spending very little.

You can create warm traffic items with some of your slower selling products or new bundles that involve hot items—these will work great for warm traffic. Setting up a deal will help to move them along your buyer's timeline. This is the assistance that you would be giving them. Warm traffic should be in their own categorized list as they first into your database. Moving each contact along as they choose to purchase and then taking them down the next phase of the buyer's timeline.

Lastly, we have gotten to the point of "Hot Traffic." The best kind, right? Cold traffic is pretty good since you get to be creative. When I think of hot traffic, I think of "monetization." These are the actual people who you can capitalize on. Is it vicious? No. This is what they signed up for. There is also a nice twist, since they pay the most, they get offered the best products. So, it's a win/win. With hot traffic, you now have committed customers, who opened their wallet, which shows trust and loyalty toward your business. So, don't break it! Keep them satisfied by offering exclusive content and premium products. You can sell all your high-ticket items and open the platform for newly made Monetized traffic. This is where core products are offered and premium packages will exist. This can be done all from the power of your email. You can seamlessly continue to sell directly from email campaigns at a click of a button. Allow your hot traffic to be the first to know the newest or hottest products.

Monetization is the process of earning revenue, but no one ever gets to this point without first farming your area and growing your prospects. Hot traffic wants upsells and premium content. When it comes to musicians, there are several pieces of extra content you could build around your music, such as creating merchandise that has value for new fans from an aspiring artist.

People are no longer simply buying products—they are buying into your story. They are buying into your company and what it stands for. So, you must create the imagery that will allow people to align with the beliefs and conduct that you choose to emulate.

Activation, acquisition and monetization are elements of selling and creating revenue that is a three-part mechanism. None can happen without the other; it's a marriage (*Married with Children* theme song just popped in my head). So, you need to understand the reasons why you are building your email list and have goals associated with doing so. If you do not envision your endgame, then you cannot be effective at marketing your business to its full potential.

Chapter 4

What is Marketing Automation?

If you're thinking this is a lot of information so far and it sounds like a hassle, well, yes it all can be, initially. This is not an easy task, but everything takes effort and sacrifice if you want to be good at it. The positive thing is that once you get through your initial setup of content, products and emails, then you can use it as an automated system for the most part. With inbound marketing, people often run into problems doing so much all at once. This is true, especially if you are a marketing specialist for a company, and you are a one-man show who is doing so much on your own and not having any leverage for redistribution of work. Grand expectations yielding low results, everything becomes overwhelming and difficult to keep up. It hits as information overload. If you currently find yourself on work overload or think you will be after this, the good thing is you can automate much of your marketing to work on its own.

Automation works through the process of being able to build enough content to continually run time and time again. Think about how often you release content, then you decide to begin a scheduling process. You schedule your emails and you plan your social media posting for it to run with content any time you wish even when a computer or phone isn't accessible. Always get your content in working order with scheduling management resources, like *Later.com* or *Hootsuite.com*. If you are looking for email carriers, some of the best I have worked with are *clickfunnels.com, getresponse.com, mailchimp.com* and *mailerlite.com*. These sites allow automated emails, tracking, and flexible scheduling. You can even set up auto-replies.

Now, real engagement is still needed, and you want to give the personalized human touch by communicating with people and answering questions. Automation is to let you have an extra leg to stand on. Schedule posts or messages out to relieve and lessen time constraints. It never ends well when you're trying to put two hands in ten places. Multitasking is good, but every person has their limitations. I had to discover this the hard way.

Marketing automation can take place from driving traffic to selling products. What you need to keep in mind is the building of content. You will have to create templates that have a series of predetermined responses for you to create automated content. Automating can happen on social media as well. Content management will be something that you will want to adapt to and learn to control, and once you have this underway, you will have a powerful marketing tool. Repetitive tasks now become easier, freeing up much of your time to get back to being creative rather than administrative. There are several ways that marketing automation can work. Large companies choose to work with extensive software, but you can get the same results by using scheduling systems within your preferred platforms.

This takes us into our next step utilizing powerful tools of automation. Create a social selling avenue within your email list. Sending out email campaigns is one thing, with specific results that can't always be determined. There is also the formula of walking a customer down a specific funnel and converting them from cold to hot—all in a sequence of steps.

Chapter 5

Understanding Drip Marketing

D rip marketing is the process of walking a prospect through a series of selling funnels in order to help them make a purchase. Automating this process is one of the largest factors in having it work successfully. When someone signs up to join your email list, you'll want to have a scheduled automated message that serves as a greeting to welcome them for subscribing. Now, even if sales don't result in this initial introduction, it's a start of a process. This system is built not to look for a hard sale on your first email. Your goal is to create an introduction and an interest. You'; want to inform and educate the prospect on what they just signed up for.

The idea behind drip marketing is to offer a personalized email that directly speaks to the prospect. This is where those relationship building skills will come in handy. Creating transparency between who you are and your interest in the prospect is crucial.

Your first email should briefly inform who you are and your intentions. These prospects can still receive other emails outside your drip campaign, which will create special relationship building techniques.

In drip marketing, you can let clients know about special offers like, live broadcasts, interviews, podcasts and webinars along with products that support this content. Depending how the prospect answers, they can be funneled through different lists that engage them with different automated emails within your drip campaign.

The main idea is to stay engaged with each prospect's needs and effectively zone in on them. Create useful content that is specific to individual needs. How they engage with your content should give you an idea of everyone's interest. If you're marketing on social media, you may find difficulty in interrupting the natural flow of people's content by leading them off the platform. To combat this, create a limited offer with urgency, offering enticing information on another site. You should give an "Act Now" call to action if they really want to get your offer. Your target audience should be determined early on. Just knowing your industry and what you sell is not enough. You must know what the people are looking for; you learn this through the questions prospects ask. When people have problems, they ask questions. Therefore, it's all relative that you know what inquiries they're asking so that you can have the right solutions. Drip marketing successfully answers a series of questions by knowing about the prospect. You know why they are here; you know what they are looking for.

If you have products or services you want to sell on the Internet, create a website where you'll advertise what you're offering. Begin by spreading the word about your products or services to the world. You can easily and quickly do this via email. Email marketing is certainly one of the most powerful strategies in digital marketing. It's quick, cost effective—you don't pay a set price for every email—and allows you to contact people in all parts of the world. As a result, you can get more purchasers and respectively more revenue for less investment.

How does one accomplish bulk email marketing campaigns?

You can use online bulk emailing services, or you can pay a marketing firm to do your bulk email promotions, or you can use direct email marketing software to distribute your email campaigns.

Using software can be the most cost-effective method if you have the time to manage your prospects list and accomplish your email campaigns with a constant frequency.

There is a wide choice of direct email marketing software packages available online. Some are even freeware programs that don't require any investment. Although they don't generally have the value-added features that come with software packages that you purchase; however, if you aren't running a large email marketing campaign, they may suit your needs for accomplishing specific tasks just fine.

What is Drip Email Marketing?

The concept behind drip email marketing consists of sending periodic emails to prospects and clients, hoping to bring them to your website and make them purchase products or services. It is an effective method to generate new purchasers from your prospects and keep relationships with your existing clients.

Drip email marketing is a result of the idea that no one purchases online products or services instantly. A visitor can come to your website a few times before becoming a purchaser. Keeping this in mind, how are you going to stimulate your prospects' interest to your site? How will you keep them informed about your products and services? This is why a drip email marketing campaign is effective and gets to the point.

Imagine that a prospect has just visited your site and you don't have anywhere for them to leave their contact information. Early on, you should add a sign-in form to your web site to collect the prospects' email addresses. It's rather useful if your sign-in form asks the subscriber to provide some additional information and not only the email address. I'm not talking about confidential information. I'm talking about the subscriber's area of interest, such as hobbies, specific needs, or at least the emails he/she prefers to receive, whether text or HTML. All this information will help you segment your prospects and send more relevant email messages to each group.

So, based on new subscribers' preferences, you set up a drip email marketing campaign catered to their specific needs. Each message you send gives more information through their inquiries and slightly hinting at your products or services. It is an important way to stamp your name in their mind. Remember, you don't sell anything yet. You just give advice and information toward their needs.

For your existing clients, a drip email marketing campaign is similar. You only need to tailor the emails so that they are oriented to the client after a purchase goes through. Your email drips must contain relevant information that can help the customer with the products or services they purchased. The customers must be sure that you are always there to assist them. When your client believes that you are a faithful and reliable partner, they will be ready to purchase from you again.

I'm sure you can feel like you'll need several tools to accomplish your drip email marketing campaign. But you can find many SaaS (software as a service) options online that can handle your growing list of prospective and current clients. Your email management software must be flexible enough to treat each client or prospect according to the routine and strategy of your drip email campaign.

Another thing to remember about drip email marketing is that you must not send meaningless emails. Each message must have either informative content, or a real reason to contact your prospect, not just a note saying "Hi!" or "How are you?" That can work if it's followed by some substance or call to action.

If your drip marketing email cannot keep the clients' interest, they will delete it immediately, and the next time you send them a message, they might also move that to their trash inbox. We all are busy people and won't spend our time reading dull messages. If you are trying to build a relationship based on trust, you cannot tolerate that they never open your emails. You can start directly from the subject line. The subject itself must grab people's attention and make them want to read your message. This is the essential concept behind a drip email marketing campaign—to develop a trusted relationship with your customer by sending valuable information. When the rapport of informative and useful emails is established, your clients and prospects will be looking forward to every email from you, and they will even recommend your company and your products to others. They will thank you. Isn't that exactly what you want for your business? I'm sure it is. That should be your consumer end goal.

Chapter 6

Aiming for Viral Marketing

The term "viral marketing" was originally referenced in Greek Athenian histories and finally coined in the late 1990s by venture capitalist Steve Jurvetson. The term viral marketing is commonly defined as network-enhanced word-of-mouth.

Viral marketing is considered very similar to network marketing. It is proven that the typical Internet user is very vocal about their online experiences. So, in this way, for each person you reach, you will be reaching a group of friends. Viral marketing is all based on their vocal online experiences. A typical example of viral marketing is a reputed firm sending out, for example, birthday greeting cards. At the bottom of the card will be the option of giving the card to the sender or to anyone else you might like. This is viral marketing in action! Or if perhaps you have a newsletter, or write articles for some newsletter, then you could add a line at the bottom of the article saying, "Know someone interested in this? Click here to email it to them," which hopefully results in another prospective client to view your newsletter link.

Viral marketing is considered like a virus carried over the Internet to various web hosts or people. This virus is stealthy, patient and cunning, and is a very cost-effective way to generate awareness of a product or service to the audience. Basically, a viral campaign is said to scale easily from small to massive. This means that a campaign can start with only ten people affected through marketing. These ten people then tell another ten friends and family each, until it gains traction at a hundred people plus who each know another hundred people and lets them know about the product. This is sure the lowest cost means of advertisement, and if it's delivered organically, then that means no money was paid for ads (in the traditional sense). Viral marketing can take place in the existing marketing platforms that we all use. Viral marketing is a great means of giving away valuable products through a series of content to the general audience. Not only that, the viral message takes advantage of other resources.

Learning about viral marketing may inspire you to create your own viral campaign for marketing.

However, to create viral content, you must understand what constitutes a successful way of exponentially spreading your message. To create a success, you must creatively originate content that's authentic. Once you've determined your viral content, knowledge of how it can spread must be learned. The most important thing to remember is that the email, website, application or video being shared must be unique and informative. This is one of the foundations of content becoming viral. It must originate from a credible entity, otherwise it will be mistaken as blatant advertising and immediately discredited. Finally, if the takeaway message on the website does not resonate with the target audience, then it will be a waste of time.

Viral campaigns usually have three stages: seed, germination and growth. Similar to plants needing the seed to be of quality genetic material to thrive and then germinating and receiving proper nutrients to grow. Viral marketing requires this same treatment because it must start with a great campaign that grows with its advertisement through word-of-mouth or in a grass roots manner. However, there are situations in which viral marketing fails. The reasons for failure are usually due to incompatibility with the brand, irrelevance to target audience, unrealistic expectations and lack of sustainability. So, remember, if the campaign contradicts core brand attributes, or doesn't map to existing marketing objectives, the viral marketing will fail.

If the message of the product does not resonate with the target audience, then failure within the campaign exists.

Let's take a detour and discuss how your mailing list can support a viral campaign. For all this, one can design an email newsletter for the marketing if needed. The newsletter must, like other newsletters, have a detailed description of the product to be marketed. Then there can be graphics to enhance the look of the newsletter, but black text on a white background gives terrific response from the audience. There should be a subscription link in the newsletter, so the prospective buyer can subscribe to the newsletter if interested. The contact information is important since it allows you to send the potential customer an email and announce any new product you may have!

You first want to get started by looking for an email marketing company that fits your needs and your budget.

There are many out there. From Mailchimp, ConstantContact, GetResponse, MailerLite, VerticalResponse.

There are several out there. This can take you some time to get through. You want to go with what gives you the best bang for your buck. Some key features you would want to look for is, auto responding, landing pages, form building features and more. You want to make sure that you can send an elevated level of emails and collect a decent number of contacts. Usually being able to send an unlimited number of emails to your first 1,000 contacts is a good way to start.

I enjoy the features of MailChimp and MailerLite out of most email marketing services. They seem to be the most cost friendly with the most features. The autoresponder is the main feature that is going to really help you to build out your email system. The autoresponder feature will allow messages to be sent to people in a periodic time, based on your preference.

For instance, if someone signs up for your email list, you can create an automated message that will reach them in the first hour, or after the first day, two days or a week if you'd like. The point is to set up a series of these messages that contact someone with the series of drip marketing steps you design. You can have emails that reach someone based on very specific choices. For example, if you have a call to action within an email, asking someone to click on a link or watch a video, or even make a purchase. Once the individual makes the given choice, they can be moved to a given list that will categorize them differently within your database. You can have automated emails that go out to people based on the choices that they make. This makes the email flow seem very natural and engaging.

Most email marketing providers today offer the feature for personalization. The personalizing effect allows you to address each person by first name. Granted, you're collecting this information upon initial contact. If you send out 500 emails surrounding a single topic, each person will be addressed personally by first name. You can customize your messages to create more intimate conversations with each person in your contact list. You want people to get to know you through that level of transparency This is the foundation for building a solid brand and eventual viral messages. You are also inviting them in to be a part of the world you're creating. You do this by making them feel that you are getting to know them.

Write down what it is that you want to focus on. Find out what you want to capture. If you are working in the music industry, think of other offers that you have surrounding your music. What information can be interesting?

What merchandise can you push that's unique? How can you make your fans feel immersed? You can offer exclusive information for the die-hard fans. This may mean offering backstage access to your live shows. Or planning rallies for free tickets or releasing exclusive music and videos.

This is an extremely powerful tool because you have full control of what you can offer hundreds or thousands of fans time and time again. There are endless features that you can work within email marketing providers. You need to have a system built that walks your fans/prospects through a buyer's timeline leading to an end goal that turns to profit. The end goal should be a deal that you do not offer anywhere else on the Internet. This is a step-by-step process in which you build free to low- priced products that eventually turns to larger core products.

Keep enough inventory on hand and drive enough traffic within your email system that you are creating sales and a fan base.

If you are a business that is carrying physical products, inventory is something you want to keep in mind. Especially when it comes to email campaigns that may offer flash sales and other high demand promotions.

When you think of an email system, think of how you want it organized. Decide the layout first before you begin to jump in. Every email should be delivered with purpose and intent. What I mean by that is, you should always work on educating through your email and leading the reader to act. The action doesn't always have to be to purchase, but it should be to further engage with more material and getting used to making decisions within your marketing campaigns. A great way to do this is by getting feedback. You can send out polls and surveys to allow people to engage and make decisions within your campaigns. The other benefit is you get an idea of what your prospects think and their opinions, especially how they feel about your company and products.

What you want to do is create patterns that people recognize and become familiar with. Emails are the most successful when there is a level of trust on both sides. You trust the opinion and the cooperation of your readers and they trust you through honesty and proof of concept. Without creating the trust within the system you've built, then you fail to solidify connectivity with your audience. It's one thing to have others read what you have created on social media, but it's very different to see it in their inbox since it's their own personal space.

Make sure your message is clear and your intentions are as well. Give people useful, honest information that is interesting and compelling. Know the industry that you are catering to. You really need to understand who it is you are offering information and what it is that they need. A series of emails that tackle their needs is all you should develop.

If you have a business that deals with home repair or roof remodeling in southern California, then you may want to target homeowners with older homes in non-rural areas. The best emails that you would want to send them is a list of cons to not having roof repair. *The problems with using an inexperienced contractor. The different material you can use and the durability. How to know if your roof is in compliance with your HOA.* These are some of the tidbit gems you want to share with your readers. This creates both trust and value. People are more likely to read emails if you offer solid and relevant information. You are recognized as a voice of authority within that industry. When you educate your prospects, you create educated customers. These are now people who are more aware of why they need your products and how to use them. When you do offer your products, they hold more value to the reader because you created a lot of understanding for them potentially and solved their issues. Now, imagine your commercial, ad or campaign using this technique with a viral outcome. The results can't be easily quantified.

Chapter 7

Understanding the Lead Magnet

We have spoken a lot about prospects, fans and readers being able to follow our content and engage with it. Where do these leads come in? How do I have them drop into my email marketing provider? Well, there are several ways to really zone in and have them jump into your database. First and foremost you want to have a lead magnet. The lead capture is your compelling email form that you will use for emails to come to you.

Some of the areas lead magnets are implemented can be on social media pages, blogs, landing pages or websites. All areas where prominent levels of activity can or should take place. Think about it as an open house sign for a realtor. You want to create your lead magnet somewhere in a high traffic area that invites people to inquire. You may want to have something even stronger than an invite; you may want to compel people to inquire. The lead magnet can become your single most important tool that you use.

The headline and subject should be written in a way that piques immediate interest. Also, offers a solution by inquiry to an immediate problem. It's wise to become specific and create solutions for immediate needs. The form that pops up on any website you visit asking your name, email and other information. The form that may be on a landing page telling you reasons why you should fill it out. These forms are information funnels providing you with valued content in exchange for your contact. Building out a lead magnet isn't a difficult task. Rather, building a successful lead magnet is where you should focus your goal.

The best way to start is by looking at forms that are in a similar industry to yours. What issues are people dealing with? What pains are they experiencing? How can you resolve their concerns?

A lead magnet needs to address someone's pain and a solution in a simple call to action. "Less is better" is an unspoken rule for creating a concise form. Clutter and overcrowding are a turn off. Think of simplistic ways to grab attention for your audience. If you are having trouble trying to find out the right compelling text for your lead capture, do a little research. Searching Google and using the keyword tool can prepare you for increased success.

Google gives the ability to search a keyword and generate popular key phrases most people search for. You can see how many times a phrase is searched, which gives you a promising idea of its popularity. Millions of people are searching queries with questions every day. The first thing that they will acknowledge is a search result that answers their questions. Ubersuggests is a great tool that locates long-tail search terms as well.

You may want to have several lead magnets that direct to your main source. Lead magnets are useful on blogs, websites and landing pages, as well as social media sites. Your plan of attack should be developing a strong traffic base first, then add a lead magnet to gauge acquisition. Below are the many types of lead magnets.

- Sidebar Magnet: This exists on the side of a site. Usually a lead capture form that is on the upper right-hand side of a site. These are more of the traditional forms. They worked well for many email marketers and still do. Some site owners want higher conversions that promote more compelling calls to actions.

- Top Bar Magnet: This presents more of a visible capture form for when the site is first entered. This can be more distracting depending on the size, but it all is dependent on what your goal is. If you are looking for a conversion focused site, you may want to put your lead capture form in the most visible area.

- Pop Out Magnet: This has become one of the most popular magnets for capturing emails. You may have seen it before—you get on a site and within seconds, a pop-up appears offering you something in exchange for your name and email address. This might feel intrusive, but remember, people are on your site because they are interested in what you could potentially offer them. What usually creates success with this method is offering a free product as an incentive for people joining your list.

Those are just a few of the many different types of lead magnets that are available.

These are also the most common ones that you will see on most websites. Even with having lead magnets set up to begin a funnel for your email marketing, this is still a small piece to a greater plan. The right lead magnet can be used to promote new products and existing products.

Your lead magnet should always reinforce your brand. Allowing it to create value and further establish brand recognition. What you offer should be perceived value in the eyes of the lead/prospect. Use this as an opportunity to test new products, campaigns and ideas with a portion of newer leads.

Using Dedicated Email Drops

There can be high rewards when gathering an email list. They call it a company's gold mine for a reason. Several different avenues are available to use when you start to build your email list. Sometimes the traditional ways of marketing, such as expecting magical results from people signing up, don't pan out. One way that companies gain their followers is through borrowing the list of companies in a similar industry.

Businesses will lease their email list time to time at a fee, allowing another organization to promote whatever they need. With stipulations varying from business to business. This is a great win sometimes, but it can become quite costly. There is no rule with what amount a company can charge for their dedicated email lists, also known as a drop list.

You can promote to an entirely new customer base, gaining new interest and followers to start building your list quickly. Having clickable links and interesting artwork helps when you are having your email promoted in someone's drop list. You want to convince people who clicked in the email to go over to your lead magnet. This way you can collect them on a list of your own.

Some things that you may want to ask about any drop list that you are using is to know who the targeted leads are in the list. You want to have them verified for list legitimacy. You want to also know how often the list is updated. The whole purpose of paying someone for use of their list is for it to be effective. No one can guarantee results, but you should have the chance to promote to the most legitimate and updated list as possible.

Metrics are also important once any list has been used. It's important to get the click-through rate, the open rate, conversion and more. You want to see how many people on the list you were able to connect with. You can measure this against how many new leads you received through your lead magnet. When you use a drop list, you should create a special lead magnet that is just for that drop list. This way you can measure the marketing campaign of the drop list and see how well the conversions have done without it being mixed with any of your other traffic.

Dedicated email drop lists usually come in the form of advertising. You want to look to see if they give advertising opportunities in their announcements or newsletters. You can typically find this on the side or bottom of a website. Not all email advertising means that you will have exclusive (dedicated) emails, so you need to email the company and ask specifically. Getting any exposure to a new audience is beneficial. You just want to make sure that the list is targeted to your interest and demographic.

Websites like *WharRunsWhere.com* can offer guidance on similar sites that your competitors may be advertising on and receiving success. Most of the time if they are ranked next to the site, which you are currently looking to purchase, your chances of obtaining a dedicated email drop list are high. Getting good leads comes with a price, so make sure you get this from a valuable source.

Chapter 8

Developing the Automated Process

Wouldn't everything be easy if all your marketing was automated? You didn't even have to touch anything, and it worked for you. Getting your email process down to a limited or single button click becomes most effective when everything begins to work on its own. This is a true "drip" process for marketing. Once you master a well put together drip marketing process, you'll end up having complete control over your business. You will never have pure exact results forecasted, but with an automated process, you can get a close figure on your metrics based on what you filter in.

Scheduling will become a necessity in making your automated marketing work. Inside most of the popular email marketing tools is the ability to schedule your emails.

You can create emails that target new prospects, social media, gender or location. This will all depend on the level of analytics collected by demographic. Each email system will vary. Starting with what you want your email system to do would be good. Write out a list of functions that you would want to focus on. Start with welcome emails, product announcements, promotions and ambassador opportunities. You can choose to contact people by specific days and schedule ahead of time so that they can receive the information on your intended date. Automated emails will help increase productivity while simultaneously taking on a larger scale project. It's like creating an extra set of hands.

Make sure that you follow the metrics on how your automated marketing will be working. Who you are bringing in and if you are getting a sufficient CTR (Click-through Rate). You can find out your CTR on the analytics area of any email marketing service that you choose. This will let you know how effective your email is. You also want to double check that the email you're sending goes to the correct audience.

Planning creates proper preparation for well-thought-out emails. Depending on your industry, you can have an email blast set for a whole month as you gather enough information. This is where you want to pull from other idea influencers about information that may be important to your audience. With enough information, you can have emails being sent to your list on a regular basis. Creating relationships where you become attentive to leads through your lead magnet.

People do not join your email list to be forgotten. They are looking for the same content they were enticed with. So, make sure you have your automated emails ready within a sufficient time.

I usually like sending the first email within an hour. It seems an hour will give them enough time to see it's real. Your automated messages all need to sound genuine, and not automated. Your messages should authentically "speak" your voice.

Think to yourself—how would you want to greet people if you had a brick and mortar shop and they walked through your door? What's your business model? Some companies have kept a very formal approach even in the changing times while other companies have taken a business casual approach.

This creates an at ease environment like you're in someone's home. It also gives off a more relaxed feeling. These business owners are usually great hosts.

A digital introduction should be the same way you want people to feel like you are providing the experience they're looking for. Automated isn't about the quantity of customers, it's the quality. Take the time to create an exclusive experience.

Customer experience is everything, especially online, because once you lose them, they don't come back. Walk them through a process that reveals in each email information they don't know but should. Something they are not doing but should be. . Something that they are lacking and you can offer to fill that void.

Reaching out to customers isn't the only way that automating your emails can enhance your service. Your time is valuable and can be used effectively when you have an effective tool to automate certain processes. Establishing an automated system in place allows you to have time to focus on other parts of your business. Being able to properly correspond or follow up with people isn't rocket science, but it can become tedious and time-consuming. You must remember you are opening up dialogue to begin building relationships. These relationships are based upon follow-up; people want to be contacted within a reasonable amount of time. The saying, "Out of sight, out of mind" is very common because when people don't hear from you, they forget about you. Especially if someone is showing interest in wanting to spend money or has recently purchased, your response time should be within that same day. Your emails need to work as an extension of yourself when you are not available. Creating a timely response shows that the purchase mattered, and you were not just eager for them to purchase without further communication.

Even when you have available time, you will still find yourself with a lot of tasks to do that will support and scale your business. Fulfilling orders, customer support, handling an FAQ and all sorts of things. The important part of all of this is trying to find balance between the services you offer and on the time you can commit. Also, another part for automating emails is to help you monetarily. You will increase your revenue quicker because you can service more people by having a system in place. Keep in mind that when you're crafting your emails to reach your audience, you should act more of a friend to each person you connect with. That small perspective helps to shape how you will deal with your audience. Instead of feeling each person is potential for $$$, you can instead perceive them as a person looking for advice. Play the long game. The turn for automated marketing to bring revenue can happen quickly, yet still requires time and patience. As a friend, you don't focus on selling, and instead offer them lucrative suggestions. This helps to eliminate the salesman/woman tone you may have when offering products.

A feature often overlooked with an automated email system is the opportunity to ask and receive input from many different people. You can survey your audience and find out more of who they are and what they think. This works great for trying to fit people into lists. Such as categories that you may want to run as a campaign, which can be targeted with a segmented list. You can now ask directly what your audience's interests are, follow their behaviors, and learn to understand their purchasing habits. Automation lets you track in multiple ways. Not only are you tracking by the traffic, engagement, website duration and CTR, but you are tracking directly from personal feedback. You become kind of like the government...for better or worse.

Chapter 9

Email Consistency

They say it takes 30 days to form a new habit. Well, sometimes it can even be 45. We get into learning something, but it's not always about having the knowledge. Sometimes it's about learning how to have a routine. However, it's a challenge to find a way to fine-tune repetition in our head with what we do in business. This is another important key point to what you'll need to know. Every process that you choose to put together needs to be met with repetition. The way the mind works is nothing short of the word "unbelievable" and "genius." The way we operate as human beings for the most part can be the complete opposite.

Especially when we look at what we are dealing with today. So much is thrown at us, as far as distractions, which makes everything difficult. People are in a place of being busier than they have ever been. More parents are working and more people are hostage to technology, along with media pumping out at an exuberant rate. So, when you send an email or you contact someone and it's only one or two times, you can't expect them to want to buy into your story or buy what you're selling. They need to hear from you a few times, and you need to be consistent. So many companies come around, like a fly-by-night, and merely want someone to buy what they sell and then be gone.

People need consistency for mainly two reasons: One, is to be reminded, and two, is for trust. Without understanding these attributes, you have already lost in your race to build a flourishing email business. If you want to throw a third attribute out there, then this one's for you. Number three is patience. Patience with your audience, your email and building your list. It will unfold, and it will happen, but you must calm down the uneasy eagerness. Because that "I want it right now" feeling of expecting results immediately will just mess up your level of clarity. Focus and stay consistent, and allow them time to think and decide whether they'll consume what you're selling. Once the formula is finalized and the first few people start catching on, then you have opened the floodgates. This entire process should be a rinse and repeat process.

Sometimes people don't get the email the first time around for whatever reason. When they see it finally coming in, it can draw curiosity.

How you end up being consistent is also paying attention to your audience's behaviors, learning their peak hours. This will tell you the prime time to send messages because you will see when you are getting the highest level of attention and engagement. When people can rely on receiving information from you during their highest engagement times on the Internet, you are putting yourself into a peak time.

You want time, consistency, and an automated system in order to have the process work for you. Your audience, whether it be prospects or repeat customers, to feel important. This is human nature. It's your role to ensure you're fulfilling your audience's sense of importance and belonging. If you want them to give you some of their time and possibly their money, then you have to offer value on a consistent basis. That also sets the tone of letting you know that they are important to you. Even if it's a subtle email that checks in with your audience and gives them useful advice to help them through their day.

There are certain times during the day when it is easiest to reach people, so you want to keep in mind both domestic and international time zones. Paying attention to the time will help you know when to send emails to maximize reach. You never know when someone starts to expect your message once they incorporate it into their routine. Your diligence pays off when people take notice of your work and how you put it together. Often, I start a schedule that can last an entire month, which entails planning what the emails will be, what will go out and what holidays to incorporate. This helps to plan out a schedule to minimize the spontaneous factor. Most likely you will end up working in two-fold. You will have automated messages that respond to those who have contacted you, and you will also have automated emails that are proactive with contacting your existing list.

Remembering these characteristics will help you stay on track. Competition is extremely heavy but easily detoured when you have services and a work ethic that are superior to another business.

Chapter 10

Developing Great Content

Consistency, social media, automation, drip marketing are strategies toward successful email marketing. You're probably wondering how email became so sophisticated and how you can create an effective functioning machine. For the most part, you have learned what many services do, but we haven't focused too much on determining what is right for your needs. There are a variety of ways that email can work for you. You just need to know how to put it together.

The saying that most people fall back to is "Content is King." That's because it is and comes from the saying "Cotton is King," which was abundant in southern states as one of their main exports. Content, in the digital world, is a major export. It is the life blood of all marketing. Without content, we have a void and open space filled with unmanifested ideas. It'd be like watching a football game without any players. We need content. This is where getting familiar with who your target audience is fundamental. There are so many ways that you can take a single content model and craft it to be a multitude of different pieces. This can be a very fun part of all the things that you put together because you start zoning in on your creativity and what makes you unique. There are usually five distinctive ways of distributing content to your audience. It's up to you to find out which ones they're most receptive too. You can do any of the following:

1. Written

2. Audio

3. Images

4. Video

5. Streaming

There are five major ways content can be delivered. We will cover written, audio and streaming for this chapter.

All these methods can work in conjunction with each other or be equally independent. They also need to be seen for a powerful individual tool as well. Understanding how digital technology works, along with marketing, can create content in a very effective manner.

With the rise of media driven content and the advancing of technology, written work in the eyes of many has fallen by the wayside. But, just like the power of emailing, this is far from true. Written content is the life force that gave birth to the digital realm. Writing is the glue that binds all content together. Therefore, it's important to focus toward reaching your audience in some written form.

Every piece of content online is only playing a part of one massive stage. Each form of content can be imagined as actors in one giant theater. When you pull back the curtains and look at what pulls the strings, you would see the web is full of millions of words strung together, forming a beautiful instrument. This is what some of the largest platforms online understand. Keywords and metatags strung together to create a searchable index. Algorithms put into place to recognize the behavior and patterns in written words. Written information is what gets you found. That is why all the large media outlets online are still reporting in written format because it creates a large amount of relevancy. Yes, you should always want to tell an interesting and compelling story for your audience.

What a journalist looks for, on top of breaking a relevant news story, is curating a high-level of engagement. When you get people talking, you have content that gains traction.

You should check with any keyword tool to find out what in your industry gets searched for each month. How many people are looking within your industry and what keywords are they using? Take it a step further and curtail the search to your local geographic area. Start by dominating the online searches within your zip code or a niche within your city blocks. This is your chance to change the narrative if you choose. With knowing the right information about your audience, you also know how to bring great stories to their attention, with words that pique the interest of the search engines. This all falls in line with what is known as SEO (Search Engine Optimization). Written information is the kind of content that search engines recognize the best. This is a major factor for your newsletters and email blasts. If they get shared, you want them to be search-friendly to increase the exposure of your content. Written content is the lifeline for all content marketing. You can go to *Moz.com*, Ubersuggests or use Google AdWords keyword tool in order to get a deeper look at who is searching specific keywords. Ubersuggests allows you to see articles written by those keywords and the activity that was received on those articles. The headline that was used and how the search engine ranked those keywords.

Using hashtags helps to assist with a lot of content being shared. Sites like Instagram, Twitter and Tumblr strongly rely on the hashtag system. *Hashtagify.me* is a good site to look at what the latest trending tags are to increase your content reach.

Content is all about visibility, and allowing your content to be seen is what will pull people in. Make sure that you take each arena of content as important as the next. Every area of content has its strengths.

Let's now talk about audio. We as musicians see this as one of the deepest levels of content. Audio is another great way to market and get people to hear what you have to say. This is especially effective for emails, even though playing audio within an email isn't always ideal. In emails, you can direct your subscribers through a link where your audio can be heard. Audio can communicate emotion, feeling and education in a variety of ways that you don't always get in written format. A lot of times audio can be split into a public outlet of marketing content, and it can also be a very intimate and private thing as if someone is speaking directly to you.

Audio is not only great for music, but it's great for podcasts, teleconferences, meetings, tutorials and much more. A podcast is one of the more common and successful ways of using audio. Podcasts allow you to build an audience and engage people on a regular basis. With so many audio streaming services available, it's easier to find outlets to use your audio content.

Audio has a key role in content and the way that it's shared, especially for musicians. The way audio has become digitized has even changed music's format in a drastic way. Music went from physical to digital downloads and now to streams.

The streaming generation has become the main way music is received. Artists are using streams to earn an income and market their creative work. Streaming is now on the forefront of how music or audio is being shared all together. If you observe around you, you'll notice how often someone is attached to a digital device, especially young people. Streaming is one of the most common ways of listening to audio vs. Downloading. Streaming sites have become extremely important in being able to reach people on the go and musicians can earn income from the service itself. Given streaming popularity, this equates to another way content could be delivered.

Chapter 11

TAILORING YOUR MESSAGE

Promoting our businesses or organizations with emails is essential for a lot of reasons. You see email marketing is very dynamic. You can make the mails that you intend to send so tailored and personalized to the peculiarity of your prospective clients. It is ideal that we can prospect a large range of social groups and adjust the message suitably. With the ever-occurring dynamism in the world of business, both locally and globally, it is imperative that we develop the gut and aptitude to react rapidly to every progression that the world of business has to offer. One of such is "email marketing."

You know, the Internet has no limits, and this implies that your email can get to anybody, anywhere on planet Earth. Should your business have inclinations to work far and wide, then, this is the real thing. This is the diamond you have been looking for all along. In addition to that, there is ideally no one who doesn't look forward to having some tangible business and individual success. Whatever your online outlets are, numerous advertising modules for email marketing you are available should you take advantage of it, which will immensely help you make the best of your prospecting and certainly open you to new realms of possibilities and success.

The customer's specificities (or should we call it peculiarities?) are of utmost importance in email marketing. These peculiarities will help us know what content our customers are searching for.

There's a well-known saying that goes, "You never get a second chance to establish a first impression," and this is just the key set of words in email marketing. You have got only split seconds to make that impression, hence, the pressure is on you to make it count.

Sadly, if you do mess it up, you may never get another opportunity.

So, perhaps the most ideal way to stand out enough and get the necessary attention that your business or organization desires is by customizing your email message.

It helps you establish a tangible connection with your prospect, which can serve you and your business well much later.

In addition, the seemingly unending task of filtering through messages has molded individuals to dispose of anything that doesn't originate from an unmistakable companion, or relative, or obviously does not open with a personalized welcoming. Any mail that doesn't allude to the recipient by name goes to the spam folder—never to be opened again. Hence, it is ideal to be on a first-name basis with the email recipient. You'll get further in the entryway, with a higher possibility of having your message opened and read.

Once you are sure you have captured your prospect's attention, come to the heart of the matter. Enticing your client through customized messages without hitting the nail on the head in good time can be counterproductive. You may get the individual angry and entirely irritated, hence, crumbling everything you have put together like a stack of cards. Communicate what your email promotion is about quickly. Virtually everyone hates reading long, directionless messages.

It's essential to customize a welcome and convey a brief message that is anything but difficult to read and simple to comprehend. In any case, significantly more imperative than putting a "face" on the customized messages is adding a special identity to them. Individuals are accustomed to receiving mass messages and sending them into the spam folder. You must construct an email that sounds as though it was composed by a genuine independent music artist for real people or organizations.

When putting together a marketing email, an organizational logo is not required. Customized messages should simply have the name of the individual or organization who is releasing the email message. This is fundamental to email marketing. Structure the email to appear as though it originated from you and only you. At that point, make it feel as direct as possible. With all these attributes, your message stands way above others and increases the chance of winning a space in their heart.

Trust me, a personalized message is the way to become famous, and it's your chance to brand your art. So, ensure you maximize personalization as you send your next set of emails.

Chapter 12

CUSTOMERS AREN'T NAMELESS FACES

The amazing, and yet disappointing thing about email marketing, is that this method is generally new in the domain of prospecting, and many individuals and business organizations that have yet not come to recognize it as one key path to successful business advertising, hence, the reason for the observed underperformance in many businesses. But you can start using the right way to work for your music.

Another reason for the underperformance can be the wrong kind of emailing. Some business emails read like they are from some kind of robotic algorithm.

I'm sure you don't have a scenario where somebody feels as if they received a "frame letter" that has been created by some faceless individual or organization. Such a person would quit perusing, and you will lose that prospect forever. Consequently, as an independent music artist, who is really committed to winning—it is important that you bridge this gap.

The following will help you overcome this challenge:

How Genuine?

This point can never be overstretched. As exciting as sending emails can be, we need to pay attention to details. The point here is to make the email look like it will be of immense benefit to your prospect, and of course, you must never disappoint this expectation should you win your prospect over. This is very important and worthy of note. Research affirms that mails from individuals

(e.g. tomfoster@companyname.com vs @gmail.com) have fundamentally higher readership rates than messages sent from mere company email addresses. Messages with a particular individual name attached has a higher likelihood of not being tagged "spam" by the prospect.

Again, this point can never be overstretched.

Customize Your Greeting

An anonymous faceless outgoing address will cost you more than bless you. If you know the recipient's name, why on earth will you hesitate in making use of it when giving a greeting? These are some of the little things people ignore when drafting a prospect email. It will make a difference in the greeting. Also, do ensure that the rest of your email message is similarly as important.

Customize the Look and Master the Perception

Having a customized email and unique layout will also do a lot of good. In case you are sending mails for the purpose of winning music video sponsors over to your side, it is important to ensure that the look of your email format communicates most suitably. Should your messages constitute a whole of small and similar lead supporting promotions, they ought to be associated by a comparable plan and an identical structure. By reflecting what you think about your clients, your messages will appear to be more commonplace and helpful to prospects.

You Can Use More of Weekends or Other than Work Days.

Lots of people and organizations send the larger part of their prospecting email messages during the week rather than send more at the end of the week (weekends). In any case, open rates for messages sent on weekends are much higher than those for email messages sent in the middle of a typical week.

Research tells us that an email sent on the second day of the week has a possible open rate of less than 60 percent while emails sent on weekend have a possible open rate of almost 70 percent. This shows how important it is to put into consideration "what time of the week" we are sending such mails.

Send more of your prospecting email messages at the end of the week and thank me later. I'm positive the success will be phenomenal.

Customize the Planning

Every organization's business cycle is unique. When you're setting up a marketing email message, it is important to ensure that the planning lines up with the average purchasing ability of your prospects. For a known client who typically takes a month to research and settle on a choice, don't bore such a client with excessive information. You can send a brief progression of valuable messages after some time to enable you to build on previous messages.

This will give you the winner in business advertising. You indeed deserve the best as an individual and as a business organization. If you have not been taking the right steps, now you know what to do. Change your promotional techniques for good and win. Let the game be in your favor.

Chapter 13:

Optimizing for Mobile Media

1. PUT YOUR WORDS TOGETHER MORE APPROPRIATELY

Ideally, the initial segment of an email message is the subject. The subject is the reason why your recipient will either read or disregard the message... This is why your email must carry a subject/tagline no matter what.

Also, even though it may seem words like "free" or "future" will probably entice the prospect to open your message, they shouldn't ever be used because it has a higher chance of your email being flagged as spam.

You can still put this to test and see what results you get.

2. LET IT BE EVIDENT THAT YOU KNOW WHAT YOU ARE DOING AND SAYING

Consider your own particular way of dealing with messages. After you've taken a glance at the subject of an email, the main sentence of the message will be basic in your choice to keep perusing. This is considerably more imperative when you consider the commonness of mobile devices today—a phone will regularly show the subject of an email and a preview of the initial concepts of the message.

Due to this element, your first sentence must be exceptionally customized to demonstrate your knowledge about the prospect. In the event that the email appears standard and generic, you can be sure it'll be discarded as quickly as possible.

3. DRAW IN YOUR PROSPECTIVE CLIENT WITH A SIMPLE INQUIRY

Do you know there is power in the use of questions? Several email marketers have not discovered the treasure in questions. The main reason you are sending an email is to eventually make a deal happen , hence you should be looking to connect with the prospect in a way that can initiate a phone call and ultimately, a personal meeting. In this way, make sure that your prospecting message moves the individual to react to you and asking questions can do this for you. End each mail with an address and possibly a phone number. You can have great questions like, "What's your greatest need at this present time?" or you can begin your message with "Are you currently so broke that you can't afford to feed yourself three times a day?"

Inquiries are a miracle, and prospects most likely will respond because you have drawn them in and communicated a question that resonates with them perfectly.

4. *TAKE ADVANTAGE OF INFORMATION GATHERING MAILS THAT HELP YOU KNOW WHEN SOMEBODY OPENS YOUR EMAIL*

You can administer such a program with your emails, so you will know which of your messages are opened. In the last couple of years, business individuals have been left perplexed as to the numerous factors that contribute to when a prospect eventually opens their email. Organizations like HubSpot Signs and Yesware do make available free trials for this kind of email monitoring. This can be the difference you have been hoping for.

Consequently, you will know when a prospect has opened your email, you have an idea of the time to expect a call and be aware of how to better prepare for negotiation. What's more, now that you can track when messages get opened, you are more at an advantage.

You know how best to channel your energy. You know who to follow up with and this helps you to be on top of your game.

We created this to be nothing short of amazing!

As you can see, this book on email marketing covers a lot more than just email marketing.

Thank you, and I wish you all the best in your endeavors into the world of digital marketing.